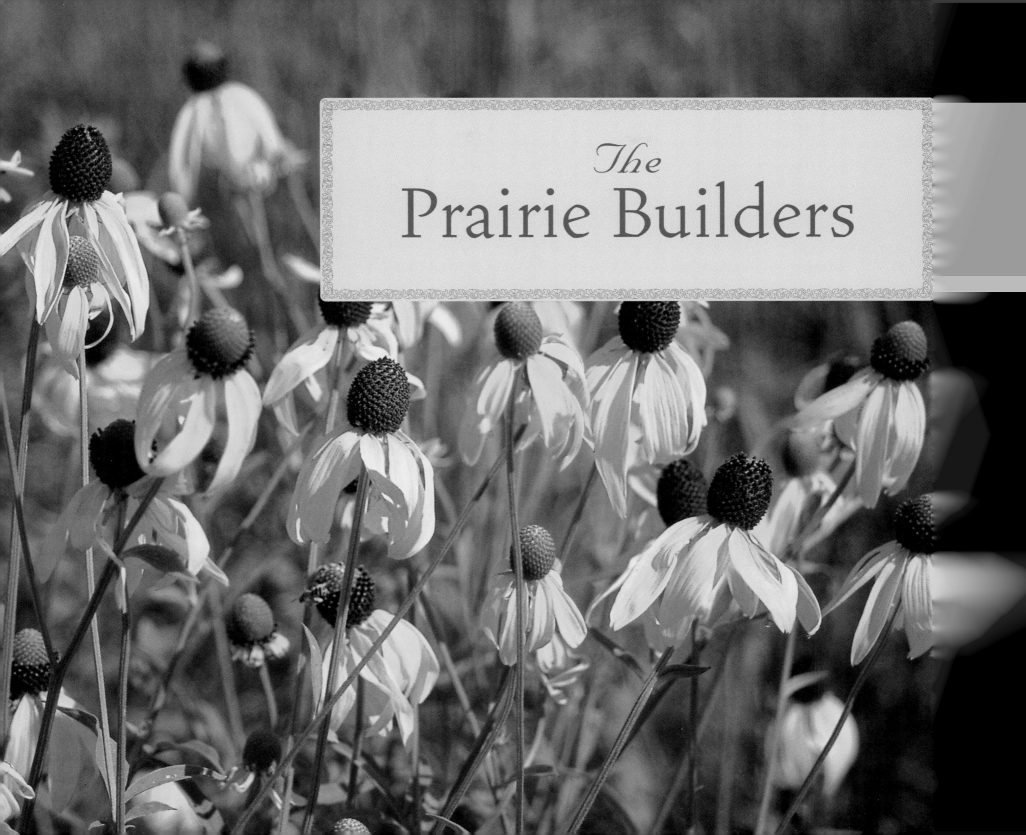

# The
# Prairie Builders

# The Prairie Builders

## RECONSTRUCTING AMERICA'S LOST GRASSLANDS

*Written and photographed by*

SNEED B. COLLARD III

HOUGHTON MIFFLIN COMPANY

*Boston*

*For Carol and Walter, my favorite backyard habitat helpers.*
*Love, Sneed*

## ACKNOWLEDGMENTS

The author would like to thank the dozens of staff, volunteers, and students at the Neal Smith National Wildlife Refuge and Iowa State University who helped me with this book. Without their kindness, interest, effort, and dedication, this story could never have been told. Extra special thanks go to Diane Debinski and her family, Pauline Drobney and her family, Nancy Gilbertson, Congressman Neal Smith, Jessica Skibbe, Jennifer Vogel, Carl Kurtz, and the entire Isaacson/Milne clan — my favorite Hawkeyes.

PAGE 1: Gray-headed coneflowers along the entry road to the Neal Smith NWR.
PRECEDING SPREAD: A tractor harvesting the prairie.

Copyright © 2005 by Sneed B. Collard III

ALL RIGHTS RESERVED. For information about permission to reproduce selections from this book, write to Permissions, Houghton Mifflin Company, 215 Park Avenue South, New York, New York 10003.

www.houghtonmifflinbooks.com

Book design by Lisa Diercks
The text of this book is set in Vendetta.
Maps by Jerry Malone

*Library of Congress Cataloging-in-Publication Data*

Collard, Sneed B.
The prairie builders / written by Sneed B. Collard III.
    p. cm.
    Includes bibliographical references (p. 70).
    HC ISBN-13: 978-0-618-39687-0
    PA ISBN-13: 978-0-547-01441-8
    1. Prairie plants—Juvenile literature.  2.  Native plants for cultivation—Juvenile literature.  3. Prairie conservation—Juvenile literature.  I. Title.
    SB434.3.C65 2005
    635.9'5178—dc22
    2004013201

Printed in Singapore
TWP  10  9  8  7  6  5

PHOTO CREDITS:
Diane Debinski: page 53 (both photos). J. Heemstra/Courtesy of Neal Smith NWR: pages 6, 12, 16, 25, 26, 30, 64. Gene Kromray/Courtesy of Neal Smith NWR: page 22. Carl Kurtz: pages 2, 8, 33, 45 (both photos), 51, 52, 60. Chris Rogers/Corbis: page 68. Kay Weisman: page 69. All other photos by Sneed B. Collard III.

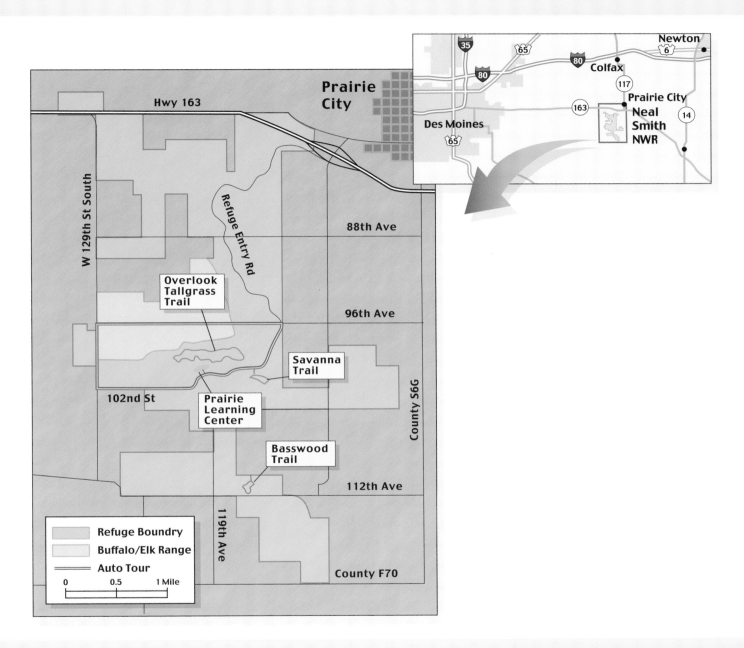

The Neal Smith National Wildlife Refuge.

# Kingdom of Fire

IT IS A FALL DAY ON THE NEAL SMITH NATIONAL WILDLIFE REFUGE IN CENTRAL IOWA. THE WEATHER IS COOL AND THE HUMIDITY IS HIGH. THE WIND BLOWS GENTLY, CREATING IDEAL CONDITIONS FOR WHAT BIOLOGIST PAULINE DROBNEY AND HER CREW WANT TO DO. STILL, PAULINE WANTS TO DOUBLE-CHECK THAT EVERYTHING AND EVERYONE IS IN PLACE. ON HER TWO-WAY RADIO, SHE CALLS THE REST OF HER TEAM. "HOW'S IT LOOK?" SHE ASKS. "EVERYONE READY? THE WIND STAYING IN CHECK?"

After a pause, a male voice responds. "We're all set."

Pauline takes a deep breath. Then she picks up a smoking can of fuel called a drip torch and shouts to several other people gathered along the meadow's edge.

"Let's go!"

Pauline and another crew member begin moving in opposite directions, dripping dabs of burning fuel onto the ground. The dry prairie grasses quickly pick up the flames. Fanned by the day's gentle breezes, a crackling orange wall five, ten, fifteen feet high quickly climbs toward the sky. Men and women carrying tools called "flappers" rush along the line, smothering stray embers that threaten to burn in the wrong direction. Two fire engines and their crews also stand ready, waiting to leap into action if the blaze gets out of control.

But today, the burn goes well. The fire stretches a quarter-, then a half-mile long, consuming any dry plant material in front of it. It churns the raw fuel into a dancing mixture of smoke, flame, and heat as it marches across the meadow.

The fire crew pauses and stares, mesmerized by the flames. But for Pauline and her team, the fire is much more than entertainment. It is a vital step in an experiment that has never been

PRECEDING SPREAD: Refuge workers set a controlled burn to stimulate prairie growth.

LEFT: Elk were once an important prairie species.

attempted before — the creation from scratch of a large, function-ing tallgrass prairie.

## THE VANISHED GRASSLANDS

The tallgrass prairie that Pauline and her colleagues are trying to create is an ecosystem that has almost completely vanished from the North American continent. Tallgrass prairie once dominated the central part of our nation. According to the National Park Service, it covered 400,000 square miles from Ohio to North Dakota and Minnesota to Texas. An explosion of plant and animal species thrived on this expanse. Grasses up to twelve feet tall fed elk, deer, pronghorn, and between 30 and 75 *million* bison, or buffalo. Native Americans, wolves, grizzly bears, and coyotes hunted this bounty. Thousands of bird and insect species also made their homes here, including hundreds of kinds of butterflies.

Amazingly, when Europeans first saw the prairie, they thought it was a wasteland and called it "The Great American Desert." By the mid-1800s, though, white Americans smartened up. They realized that the deep prairie soils would make world-class farmland. The U.S. government signed a series of treaties with Native American tribes to remove them from prairie lands and resettle them onto small reservations. Later, the government broke many of its

Farms now dominate almost all of Iowa's original tallgrass prairie lands.

promises to the tribes. It wasn't fair, but the treaties opened the way for white settlers — and the destruction of the prairie.

By the early 1900s, more than 96 percent of America's tallgrass prairie had been turned into farms and grazing lands. In Iowa, the numbers were even more dramatic. Of the 36 million acres of prairie in Iowa, less than *one tenth of one percent* survived the plow. If you imagine that the original prairie was the size of a football field, all that remained was a little patch eight feet long and seven feet wide.

Of course, when the prairie disappeared, most prairie plants and animals disappeared with it. And for almost a century, no one seemed to miss them.

### REAWAKENING

Beginning in the 1960s, though, many people gained a new concern for tallgrass prairie. They realized that most of the tallgrass prairie had been destroyed, but they began working to protect the little patches — called *prairie remnants* — that remained.

The problem was that most prairie remnants were simply too small to support all of their original plants and animals. Some remnants were a few hundred acres in size. Most were only a few acres or smaller. What were needed were some large prairies — prairies that covered thousands of acres. Prairies that stretched across the horizon.

In the 1980s, a congressman named Neal Smith spearheaded a drive to create just such a large prairie in his home state of Iowa. Iowa had lost more of its original prairie than any other state, and Congressman Smith felt that the children of Iowa deserved to know what their native land had once looked like.

"We looked for five or six years before we found the land," Neal Smith remembers. "Then one day, I received a call from an engineer at Iowa Light and Power. He told me they

Prairie remnants offer refuge to some prairie species but are too small to support many others.

Congressman Neal Smith spearheaded the effort to create a new tallgrass prairie in Iowa.
FACING: The Neal Smith NWR was created from farmland near Prairie City, Iowa, on a site scheduled to house a nuclear power plant.

had decided they were never going to build the nuclear power plant they had planned out at a place called Walnut Creek. He asked if we were interested in the land and I asked him if he could hold it for a day or two."

Congressman Smith rushed to write a bill to purchase the land along with surrounding farmland for a new National Wildlife Refuge. He got his bill passed by Congress that same year, 1989. At first, many people in the National Wildlife Refuge system opposed the idea. After all, other wildlife refuges *already* had wildlife on them, and this refuge was just cornfields. Was it possible to build a prairie from scratch? they wondered. Was it even a smart thing to do?

# What Are Prairies, Anyway?

*Prairie* is another word for "grasslands." Prairies, or grasslands, often cover the central parts of continents, where the climate is drier and harsher than near the coasts. In North America, prairie conditions are created by the Rocky Mountains, which block moist air moving east from the Pacific Ocean. Several kinds of prairies grow, depending on the amount of rainfall they receive. *Short-grass prairies* survive on as little as ten inches of rain each year. *Mixed-grass prairies* receive slightly more rainfall. Farther east, where warm, wet storms move north from the Gulf of Mexico, *tallgrass prairies* thrive on twenty-five to thirty-nine inches of rainfall annually.

Different plants and animals live in different kinds of prairies. Tallgrass prairies are especially known for their tall grasses such as big bluestem, little bluestem, Indian grass, and switchgrass. Different species of grasses and other plants flourish farther west, where conditions are drier. Over thousands of years, all of these plants have become adapted to survive drought, fire, scorching heat, and bitter cold. These same plants have also built up the rich, deep soils that today feed much of the world's human population.

BRITISH COLUMBIA
ALBERTA
SASKATCHEWAN
MANITOBA
QUEBEC
CANADA
ONTARIO
NEW BRUNSWICK
WASHINGTON
MAINE
NOVA SCOTIA
MONTANA
NORTH DAKOTA
MINNESOTA
VERMONT
NEW HAMPSHIRE
OREGON
IDAHO
WISCONSIN
MICHIGAN
NEW YORK
MASSACHUSETTS
RHODE ISLAND
WYOMING
SOUTH DAKOTA
PENNSYLVANIA
CONNECTICUT
NEVADA
IOWA
OHIO
NEW JERSEY
NEBRASKA
INDIANA
WEST VIRGINIA
DELAWARE
UTAH
COLORADO
ILLINOIS
MARYLAND
CALIFORNIA
KANSAS
MISSOURI
KENTUCKY
VIRGINIA
NORTH CAROLINA
ARIZONA
OKLAHOMA
ARKANSAS
TENNESSEE
SOUTH CAROLINA
NEW MEXICO
MISSISSIPPI
GEORGIA
ALABAMA
ATLANTIC OCEAN
TEXAS
LOUISIANA
FLORIDA
PACIFIC OCEAN
MEXICO
GULF OF MEXICO

Shortgrass Prairie

Mixed-grass Prairie

Tallgrass Prairie

Experts disagree on the original boundaries of different prairie ecosystems, but this map shows their approximate ranges.

# Under Construction

IN THE SPRING OF 1992, ARCHITECTS, ENGINEERS, AND CONSTRUC-
TION WORKERS SWARMED OVER CORN AND SOYBEAN FIELDS NEAR
THE SMALL TOWN OF PRAIRIE CITY, IOWA. SPUTTERING BULLDOZERS
BEGAN BURYING OLD FARM ROADS WHILE SURVEYORS BEGAN LAYING
OUT A NEW ROAD THAT WOULD BLEND IN WITH THE ROLLING HILLS
AND FUTURE PRAIRIE LANDSCAPE. LATER, HUGE EARTHMOVERS RUM-
BLED IN AND BEGAN EXCAVATING THE FOUNDATION FOR A NEW LEARN-
ING CENTER. AS THE REFUGE'S BIOLOGIST, PAULINE DROBNEY STOOD
AT THE HEART OF THIS SPRAWLING NEW PROJECT.

Pauline was raised in northwest Iowa, the center of tallgrass prairie country. By the time she was a child, most of the prairie was gone, but that didn't stop Pauline from growing special ties to the land around her.

"When my brothers were all home," Pauline remembers, "it was like a menagerie there. We had squirrels run-ning up and down the curtains. We had raccoons and skunks, and turtles and frogs and snakes and bats and many injured animals. People in the town would bring them to our house, because they knew we would take care of them. These days, we understand it is best to leave wild critters in the wild, but back then, people didn't think about it in quite the same way."

"Every fall," Pauline continues, "my mother and I and our family would make a foraging trip out into the countryside. It was a weed-hunting time. We would go out hunting 'weeds' — that's what we called them. My mother would find plants that looked interesting and we would come home and tie them to the rafters in the garage to dry. Then Mom would make them into these beautiful flower arrangements."

Eventually, Pauline's childhood experiences led her to become a botanist, a person who studies plants. Her first job was working in biological preserves and greenhouses owned by the University of Northern Iowa. There she learned many techniques for growing native plants — the very "weeds" that she and her mom had once searched for. Still, when she was hired to be in charge of rebuilding the prairie at the Neal Smith Refuge, she had some doubts. Could she really do it?

## FIND SEED

"In the initial days of this project," Pauline recalls, "I remember being utterly overwhelmed thinking about the dramatic human influences on the landscape. Just the *layers* of change that had happened and how we would unravel those layers or reverse them were mind-boggling to me. It has never been done before on the scale and scope of this project."

Pauline's first task was the most obvious — and one of the hardest. As work on the refuge got under way, Pauline's boss told her, "Find seed. Find ways to get it. That is what you need to worry about."

Finding seeds of prairie plants isn't easy. For many species, few — if any — of the plants have survived a century of farming and development. Also, Pauline needed to make sure that the seeds she sowed came from plants that grew nearby. A spiderwort plant from central Iowa may look the same as one from Indiana, but it probably isn't. Plants in each region

Prairie plants, such as this spiderwort, may look the same in different locations but can harbor important genetic differences.

21

have evolved different characteristics and genes. These differences may seem tiny to us, but they allow different individuals to survive in their own special surroundings.

Pauline and the refuge managers decided to limit their seed search to just thirty-eight counties that surrounded the refuge. "We hired five seed seekers, and I trained them to go out and look for certain things," Pauline explains. "These included native plants we were

ABOVE: Prairie plant survivors can sometimes be found along railroad tracks and country roads that haven't been disturbed.
FACING: Collecting seeds for the refuge using a horse-drawn seed stripper.

Congressman Neal
Smith and one of his
grandchildren sowing
seeds at Sow Your Wild
Oats Day

interested in. It also included exotic species such as leafy spurge and purple loosestrife that are nearly impossible to manage and that we did *not* want in our seed mix. The seed seekers also looked at accessibility. Could we get a seed stripper or combine into a site to harvest the seeds?"

When she sent them out, Pauline had no idea how successful her seed seekers would be, but after two and a half months, they returned with a list of more than two *thousand* sites. Many of these sites were tiny patches of overlooked land along railroad tracks or country roads. Others were in abandoned graveyards or pastures. These little sites served as mini-refuges for a variety of prairie plants.

Once they'd determined that they could collect seed from local plants, Pauline trained volunteers to begin gathering the seeds. Independent contractors also began growing and gathering seed to sell to the refuge. Getting enough seed to start planting large areas, though, would take time, and Pauline and the rest of the refuge staff were eager to get started faster than that. Fortunately, they were in luck.

### SOWING WILD OATS

"This is where it all began," Pauline says, parking her big white truck next to some old farm buildings. She climbs out of the truck and stands at the edge of a four-acre field brimming with prairie flowers. "It was 1992," she explains, "and we had some seeds that some far-sighted people had collected and donated. So I suggested we bring everyone in and plant this seed for a public event. We invited people and had our first 'Sow Your Wild Oats Day.'"

Despite rough, cold weather, a hearty band of about 150 people showed up, including the project's "father," Congressman Neal Smith. A band played and an American flag snapped in the wind, inviting anyone to come and help start the historic refuge. Then, under Pauline's direction, everyone began spreading handfuls of prairie seed and "dancing" it into the ground.

Sow Your Wild Oats Day was so much fun that it became a tradition at the refuge. And by the next spring, in 1993, Pauline's seed collectors had turned in enough seed to plant a larger number of acres. Unfortunately, that spring turned out to be one of the wettest in Iowa history.

## A WET AND WILD BEGINNNING

"I don't know if you remember 1993, but it was a huge flood year," Pauline recalls. "Des Moines made national news because the waterworks went under water. Roads were impassable. Fish were swimming in restaurants and the soil was like Jell-O. That was the year we were planting."

To germinate, prairie seeds prefer a moist seedbed but *not* being under water. Prairie seeds also like hot weather. Unfortunately, the weather in 1993 stayed cool and cloudy. As they finished planting three hundred acres of former cornfields, Pauline worried that their precious prairie seeds would never sprout. She worried even more the following two years when unusually wet, cool weather returned.

"The first two years, I couldn't find any seedlings," Pauline says. "I'd hike through the fields and find maybe one or two big bluestem grasses out of two or three hundred *acres* that we had planted. It was scary times."

But Pauline didn't give up hope, and in the third year, an astounding thing happened. All over her planted sites, prairie plants sprouted in thick, green carpets. Even the fields planted during the floods of 1993 shimmered with prairie grasses and other plants. It was a great start, but Pauline and others knew that plenty of hard work and careful management lay ahead.

Children and adults dance seed into the ground at Sow Your Wild Oats Day.

## Savanna, the Prairie's Sister Ecosystem

One reason that tallgrass prairies were so appealing to farmers was that small woodlands often grew on hillsides next to the prairie grasslands. These woodlands are called *savannas*, and they provided farmers with firewood, building materials, and forage for their livestock. Oak trees dominate healthy savannas, especially burr oak. Unlike denser eastern forests, these trees let in a lot of light, which allows an abundance of ground, or *understory*, plants to grow. Savannas support a huge diversity of life, from butterflies to bats to woodpeckers. Many animals that depend on prairies also depend on savannas.

At the Neal Smith Refuge, Pauline and her coworkers are working hard to restore savannas along with the prairies. When the refuge was started, savanna areas were badly overgrown. To correct this, Pauline and her team have cut down extra brush and exotic trees that don't belong. They've also set fires to burn away dead wood, slow the growth of invasive woody plants, and stimulate the growth of understory plants, such as this American bellflower (above right). As the savanna becomes healthier, more and more native plants and animals are returning to it — a continuing process of healing Iowa's natural landscape.

# Burnin' and Learnin'

To rebuild the prairie, Pauline and her colleagues rely on many different tools. One of the most important: fire. Many natural ecosystems need fire to stay healthy. Fire clears away dead vegetation and many larger woody plants. Fire also allows light to reach new plants, releases nutrients into the soil, and creates a blackened soil surface that warms quickly, giving plants a jump-start as they begin growing each spring.

Before white settlers arrived, Native Americans set fire to the prairies every year. The fires stimulated growth of new prairie plants, which, in turn, fed the bison and other animals people depended on. Without fire, in fact, *biodiversity* — the variety of plant and animal species — dwindles. Just a few species end up crowding out all others, and the land becomes stagnant and less productive.

To turn farm fields into prairie, Pauline and her colleagues use fire as Native Americans did. They begin by sprinkling the seeds of prairie plants across a barren corn- or soybean field. "The first year, you get a lot of weeds," Pauline explains. "These include exotic species such as red clover and Queen Anne's lace that don't belong here. But we mow the fields the first two years, possibly three, and this gets rid of many of the weeds. Beginning in the third or fourth year, we start burning whenever we can. Usually, by the fourth year, the field is looking good. Even a lousy burn invigorates native plants and promotes things in ways that wouldn't happen without fire."

One reason prairie plants survive fire so well is because most of their *biomass* — their living tissues — are underground. In a tree, most of the plant's biomass is in the trunk, branches, and leaves. Prairie plants, though, keep

about 75 to 80 percent of their biomass stored in roots hidden below ground. When fire comes, it burns away the plant's stems and leaves, but plenty of reserves remain underground to help the plant sprout again.

## NATURAL LAWN MOWERS

Mowing and fire are not the only tools for managing a prairie. Pauline and her coworkers sometimes spray herbicides on exotic weeds such as reed canary grass that are especially tough to kill. One of their most interesting tools is also the most popular with visitors: bison.

When the Neal Smith Refuge began, managers wanted to get bison onto their new prairie as quickly as possible. Bison, or buffalo, were once as important to prairie as fire. By regularly "clipping" tall grasses, bison encourage new plant growth and keep dead stems, leaves, and other fuel from choking the prairie. Bison dung also recycles important nutrients back into the soil and provides food for a variety of beetles and other prairie invertebrates.

Reed canary grass drives out many native plants, especially in wetter areas.
FACING: Like fire, mowing discourages weeds. Mowing, though, can be less harmful to certain native insects and other wildlife.

Fourteen of the giant animals arrived in 1996. Thirteen more arrived the following year. The bison were placed in a seven-hundred-acre enclosure set aside for them. A small herd of elk was also brought in. Managers weren't sure how the bison and elk would do, but the animals thrived in their new environment. In fact, they did *too* well.

In 1997, the first bison calf was born on the refuge. During the next five years, more than two dozen additional baby bison were born, along with a number of elk calves. By 2001, seventy-four bison lived at the refuge — too many for the enclosure they lived in. Refuge managers reduced the herd by donating extra bison to native American tribes so they could start their own herds. Today, managers continue to keep the refuge herd at a size that the prairie meadows can support.

Bison are natural lawn mowers — and a big hit with refuge visitors.

## SLOW AND STEADY

Despite their popularity, the bison and elk are only a small part of the story playing out day by day and year by year on the refuge. Since the first Sow Your Wild Oats Day in 1992, more than 2,500 acres of corn and soybean fields have been replaced with native prairie plants. To undertake this huge job, the refuge has a small, dedicated staff, but it also relies on hundreds of volunteers.

Volunteers collect prairie seeds, clean them, and sort them. They pull weeds and help with burning. Volunteers staff the Prairie Learning Center and help educate the public about prairies and the work being done on the refuge. The refuge is responding to this love and care. A decade ago, a visitor driving through would have seen mostly

LEFT: Volunteers Doug and Connie Maxwell collect seeds of native spiderwort plants.
RIGHT: Eighty-two-year-old volunteer Warren Burman cleans and sorts the spiderwort seeds the Maxwells collect — and tells a running stream of jokes while he does it!

cornfields and a few weedy pastures. Today, prairie grasses and flowers dazzle the eye all across the landscape.

One of the big goals of Pauline and her colleagues is to increase the diversity of prairie plants growing on the refuge. Some prairie plants, such as big bluestem grass and beebalm, are hardy and will grow almost anywhere they're given a chance. However, many prairie plants — especially the *forbs,* or "flowering plants" — grow only on healthier prairies.

To help give forbs and rarer plants a boost, Pauline raises seedlings of dozens of species in a large greenhouse on the refuge. She and her coworkers have also established an outdoor nursery where they can harvest seeds from butterfly milkweed, prairie blazing star, and other plants that they especially want to encourage.

LEFT: On former cornfields, dazzling native prairie forbs greet refuge visitors.
RIGHT: Pauline examines butterfly milkweed plants in the outdoor nursery.

# Pure Prairie Pioneers

While grasses provide the backbone of the prairie, more than 70 percent of prairie plant species are nongrasses — especially flowering plants, or forbs. Prairie flowers give the prairie its "dazzle" and diversity — and provide food and homes for thousands of species of birds, bats, and insects. Here are four forb favorites found on healthy tallgrass prairies.

▼ **PURPLE CONEFLOWER** (*Echinacea — several species.*)  Several species of purple coneflower provide nectar for many insects, including butterflies. Purple coneflower was also the most widely utilized medicinal plant for Plains Indians, who used it for everything from treating colds and reducing inflammation to soothing sore throats and toothaches. Today, millions of people around the world use coneflower — also called "echinacea" — as an herbal medicine.

◄ **LEADPLANT** (*Amorpha canescens*) Usually an indicator of a healthy, well-managed prairie, the leaves of leadplant made a popular tea for Indians and provide good forage for cattle. Indians also used the plant's soft leaves as toilet paper. Like the roots of many other prairie plants, leadplant roots penetrate deep — up to fifteen feet — into prairie soils, allowing the plant to survive drought.

▶ **COMPASS PLANT** (*Silphium laciniatum*) The compass plant gets its name from its leaves, which are often oriented in a north-south direction. This position probably protects the leaves from excess sunlight during the growing season. Compass plants are often the tallest prairie flowers, reaching heights of ten feet or more. Indian children sometimes used the plant's sap as chewing gum.

◀ **RATTLESNAKE MASTER** (*Eryngium yuccifolium*) Its name alone makes rattlesnake master one of the most popular prairie plants. Easy to recognize because of its beautiful silvery flower clusters and tough, yuccalike leaves, the plant was used to make moccasins by Indians and early settlers. The Mesquakie Indians employed the leaves and fruit of the plant in their rattlesnake medicine dance and song. Some Indians may also have used the plant to treat rattlesnake bites and scorpion stings.

## ANIMAL ACTIVITY

Plants, of course, are not the only focus of the refuge. As more and more prairie plants flourish, prairie animals are returning in greater and greater numbers. Bobcats, coyotes, badgers, skunks, deer, and the rare Indiana bat make their way through the woods and grasslands of the refuge. Everywhere you look, colorful birds forage or sing to attract mates. These include many grasslands species that were especially hard hit when prairies were destroyed, such as the Bobolink, Upland Sandpiper, and Henslow's Sparrow.

Pauline and others know, however, that many prairie plant and animal species are still missing. Hundreds — perhaps thousands — of insects, plants, and other species may have been present on the original prairie but are not there today. That's why refuge staff were so excited when a biologist named Diane Debinski came to them with an idea to bring back one of the prairie's most dazzling inhabitants.

Upland Sandpipers and Bobolinks are just two birds making strong comebacks at the refuge.
FACING: At the Prairie Learning Center, Zoe Pritchard comes face-to-face with one of the refuge's bigger badgers!

# Prairie Royalty

Dr. Diane Debinski is on a mission. It is a warm july day on the refuge, and diane climbs a hill, butterfly net and notebook in hand. A spectacular landscape surrounds her. Prairie flowers and grasses sway and tremble in all directions. In the distance, she can see the graceful prairie learning center of the neal smith refuge and, beyond that, a herd of shaggy bison grazing peacefully. But at the moment, diane doesn't care about any of that. She cares only about finding one animal.

Suddenly, someone yells, "Coming at you!"

Diane whirls around to see a large, beautiful orange butterfly speeding toward her. She swipes her net in the air and misses. Then she twirls and lunges at it again.

"Got it!" she shouts in triumph.

Her fellow butterfliers eagerly catch up with her. "Is it a Regal?" one of them asks.

Diane removes the butterfly from the net. Using special tweezers that won't hurt the insect's wings, she carefully examines her catch. Then she says, "It's a Regal."

Everyone around her whoops happily — and for good reason. The butterfly Diane holds in her hands is one of America's most beautiful and rare butterflies. This animal species, in fact, has not fluttered over this part of Iowa for more than one hundred years. The only reason it is here again now, after all that time, is because of an idea Diane Debinski came up with more than a decade ago.

## A FORGOTTEN GEM

Unlike Pauline, Diane Debinski knew very little about prairies as she grew up. She was raised in the big city of Baltimore, Maryland, and studied birds and butterflies in the wilderness of Alaska and

PRECEDING SPREAD: Diane on the trail of a Regal Fritillary.
LEFT: Diane holds a male Regal Fritillary at the refuge.

Montana. After earning her Ph.D., or doctorate degree, at Montana State University, Diane worked at the University of Kansas and then landed a job as an assistant professor at Iowa State University in Ames. As part of her job, she was encouraged to do a project that would help the people of Iowa. When Diane learned about the prairie reconstruction project at the Neal Smith National Wildlife Refuge, she started thinking about Regal Fritillaries.

One of our nation's largest and most beautiful butterflies, the Regal Fritillary used to live from the east coast of the United States all the way to the Rocky Mountains. Because of the loss of prairie and other grasslands, however, its numbers have plummeted. Only two isolated populations now exist in the eastern United States. In the Midwest, it has also disappeared from most

TOP: Diane uses special tweezers to examine a male Regal Fritillary.
BOTTOM: She marks the fritillary with a felt pen so it can be identified if it is recaptured later.

places, surviving only in small, scattered populations. Because of the Regal's beauty, size, and threatened status, butterfly enthusiasts nationwide have taken a special interest in it. So has Diane.

"I had thought about trying to restore Regal Fritillaries back in Kansas," Diane explains, "But I never got around to that work there. And then when I came here, I thought, 'Well, this is a perfect project for Iowa, where the prairie habitat is even more fragmented and the butterfly is rare.'"

One day during the early years of the refuge, Diane drove down to discuss her idea with Pauline Drobney and other refuge staff. She got a warm reception. Diane's project would help meet the goal of returning rare species to the refuge. Pauline also offered to help Diane by providing her with an intern helper and other resources. Leaving the meeting, Diane felt positive that bringing the butterfly back would be a fairly simple and straightforward task.

She was in for a big surprise.

### VERY VIOLET

Diane knew that a key to reestablishing Regals was going to be establishing the food or "host" plants that their caterpillars ate. The host plants for most kinds of fritillaries are violets. Most fritillaries can lay their eggs on or near several kinds of violets, but not

Diane studies a butterfly book at her office at Iowa State University.

the Regal. Its caterpillars are known to feed on only four species of violets, and only *one* of these — the prairie violet — grows well on the soils of the Neal Smith Refuge.

In 1997, Diane purchased about a thousand prairie violets. She also bought seeds that she gave to Pauline Drobney to begin growing violets in the refuge greenhouse. In 1997 and 1998, Diane and dozens of volunteers began planting the young prairie violet plants at several different sites. The job was much more difficult than Diane expected. "One of the most challenging tasks, that we didn't think about, is how to water the plants," Diane explains. "There you are in the middle of the prairie, digging these holes, and the soil is hard because it had been compacted for so long from farming. So digging a hole is hard, and then you have to get water to the plants."

For the first few plantings, Diane and her helpers had to haul water by hand from nearby Walnut Creek. Later, Pauline brought in a water truck to help water the fragile, fledgling plants.

Near the violets, Pauline and a team of volunteers and interns also planted butterfly milkweed and other forbs that would provide nectar for the adult butterflies. To both Pauline's and Diane's delight, the violets thrived, especially after being burned. Getting the butterflies established, though, would be another matter.

A female Regal Fritillary

## OUT OF THE ORDINARY

Diane's first idea for reestablishing the Regal was to raise its caterpillars in the lab. Many other kinds of caterpillars can be raised in cages, and Diane thought that releasing Regal caterpillars directly onto the prairie violets might be a good way to introduce them. The Regal caterpillars, though, just wouldn't survive in the lab, so Diane had to look for a different approach.

Diane decided that the only way to get Regal caterpillars onto the refuge was to bring in *gravid*, or pregnant, females and let them lay eggs near the violets. In the year 2000, Diane and her colleagues captured four pregnant Regal Fritillaries on another prairie in southern Iowa and brought them to the Neal Smith Refuge. They placed cages over violet plants and released the female butterflies into the cages. They made sure the butterflies had plenty of water and nectar, and every day, they moved each butterfly to a different violet plant.

Diane hoped that the females were laying eggs all around the violets, but she couldn't be sure. Many kinds of butterflies lay their eggs in obvious clusters directly on their host plants. Not Regals. They lay their eggs *around* the host plants and lay only one egg at a time. Regals also seem to have a special knack for hiding their eggs. Diane did find one or two eggs attached to the cages, though, and this gave her hope that the project was working.

Diane and her assistants hand-watered violet plants to make sure they would survive.
FACING: Prairie violets provide the key food for Regal Fritillary caterpillars.

The following year, she and her student Stephanie Shepherd looked for adult Regals on the refuge, but they didn't find any, so Diane decided to bring four more pregnant females to the refuge. They released the butterflies into bigger cages this time, hoping this would make them feel more at home. Diane and Stephanie also put some males in with them in case the females still wanted to mate. As another Iowa fall and winter set in, Diane waited with anticipation. Would her efforts pay off, or had she been wasting her time?

One of the smaller, original cages Diane used to house pregnant female Regals
FACING: Many butterflies, such as this Painted Lady, lay their eggs directly on their host plants. Regals, however, hide their eggs next to their host plants.

## Got Milkweed?

A prairie just wouldn't be a prairie without milkweeds. Milkweeds all belong to the genus *Asclepias*. At least half a dozen different species live on the Neal Smith Refuge. The plants play big roles in the lives of butterflies and people. The caterpillars of Monarch butterflies feed on the leaves of common milkweed. The plant contains poisons that protect the caterpillars and adult Monarchs from being eaten by birds. Adults of many butterfly species feed on the showy butterfly milkweed and other milkweed plants.

Milkweeds, though, also have been prized for their medicinal uses. Plains Indians used different kinds of milkweeds to treat respiratory problems, wounds, and even diarrhea. Early white settlers also used milkweeds to treat a host of medical problems. Don't ever try this yourself, however. Milkweeds contain chemicals called cardiac glycosides that are poisonous to people and animals.

ABOVE: Whorled milkweed
RIGHT: Common milkweed

A Gray Copper butterfly on butterfly milkweed

# Return of the Regal Fritillary

THE FOLLOWING YEAR, 2002, DIANE DIDN'T REALLY EXPECT TO FIND ANY REGAL FRITILLARIES. AFTER ALL, MANY THINGS COULD GO WRONG WITH THE PROJECT. PERHAPS, DIANE THOUGHT, THE PREGNANT FEMALES HADN'T REALLY LAID THEIR EGGS. OR MAYBE THE EGGS HAD BEEN DESTROYED BY PARASITES. MAYBE ONCE THEY HATCHED, THE CATERPILLARS HAD BEEN EATEN BY ANTS OR FAILED TO FIND THE VIOLETS TO FEED ON.

"All those things together," Diane says, "made me realize that maybe this was not a short project of a year or two. Maybe it was something that would be successful over *twenty* years."

Still, that summer, she and her students began walking through the refuge's prairie meadows, looking for Regals. They didn't see any in June, but it was still a bit early to see the adults. As June turned into July, though, temperatures warmed and Regal Fritillaries started appearing everywhere! At first there were just a few. Then Diane began to find dozens of them. "I didn't get excited at just one, since stray Regals had showed up in a few previous years," Diane explains, "but when they started showing up in large numbers, I was *elated*!"

By the end of the summer, Diane and her coworkers had counted more than ninety Regal Fritillaries on the refuge. In a place where the butterflies hadn't lived for more than a century, now they seemed to be claiming the refuge as their own.

## ONE SMALL PIECE

The return of the Regal Fritillary is great news for the butterflies and for the refuge. The Regal, though, is just one small piece of a much larger, more complex puzzle.

PRECEDING SPREAD: A male Regal Fritillary on a black-eyed Susan
LEFT: A male Dickcissel, a common colorful resident at the refuge
FACING: Beebalm, purple coneflower, and gray-headed coneflower help make the refuge look like a natural prairie, but many native species are still missing.

"We focused our project on the Regal Fritillary," Diane explains, "but not because we're obsessed with that particular species. The reason it's important is because it is an *indicator* of what's going on with the whole habitat. When you see a Regal Fritillary, it tells you a lot about the entire community of insects and plants. I don't expect to see it unless I expect to see a lot of other interesting species of butterflies as well."

This raises a key question about prairie reconstruction: If something looks like a prairie, is it really a prairie?

That is a question that concerns many people. Although the Neal Smith Refuge is beginning to look like a prairie, it is still missing many of the species that the original prairie community contained.

Refuge manager Nancy Gilbertson in front of the Prairie Learning Center FACING: The Prairie Learning Center helps visitors discover and learn about prairies and their importance.

Refuge manager Nancy Gilbertson explains, "People ask, 'Well, can't you just plant the prairie? I planted these flowers, and look, I got flowers.' But they don't understand that it's a lot more complicated than that. One prairie biologist recently discovered something like thirty different kinds of insects that were living part of their life cycles on one single plant! On that plant, he found insects he'd never seen before because nobody ever really looked. There's a whole world out there that even the best scientists don't know about and haven't yet discovered."

These kinds of stories tell Pauline, Diane, and other biologists that they have a long way to go to understand exactly what a prairie is and how it should function. But the entire refuge project also offers other insights.

One important lesson from the Neal Smith project is that we need to protect the healthy ecosystems we still have left. Even though the prairie reconstruction project is thriving, the sad truth is that it will probably never be as healthy and complete as the original prairie that was destroyed. This applies as much to prairies as it does to forests, coral reefs, and other places. As Nancy Gilbertson warns, "We need to think about what we're destroying, because we can't just plant it and get it back again."

Another important thing we can learn from the refuge is the importance of scientific research. Every day, as humans mold and shape the earth, we are making decisions that will affect future generations for thousands of years to come. As we build our growing cities and cut down forests and plow grasslands, thousands of plant and animal species are going extinct every year — including many species we don't even know we have. Science, though, helps us

The Neal Smith refuge creates an important legacy for Iowa's children. FACING: The Iowa Department of Transportation has teamed up with the University of Northern Iowa to beautify the state's roads with native prairie plants.

understand our planet and how it works. If we listen to scientists, we can make better decisions about how to live and leave our planet better off for future generations.

One final lesson of the Neal Smith project is that we humans are *part* of the world around us. Today especially, we think of ourselves as being separate from our environment, but we aren't. As Pauline Drobney puts it, "We *are* nature and our species coevolved in nature. We were a part of this system and we can't ever step out of it. If we do, the system will perish. This whole project is about the process of living as part of the land, not just about producing something separate from ourselves."

### PRAIRIES RISING

Many people in Iowa and across the United States are taking these lessons to heart. The Neal Smith National Wildlife Refuge is our nation's largest prairie reconstruction, but individuals and smaller groups are rebuilding

their own prairies almost everywhere you look. In Iowa, for instance, the Department of Transportation is working with the University of Northern Iowa to replant prairies along highways. These strips of prairies not only provide habitat for wildlife; they keep out exotic weeds that are difficult and expensive to control.

The National Wildlife Federation and the North American Butterfly Association both have programs that encourage people to replace their lawns with prairie plants and other native plants. Students across America are also planting "butterfly gardens" at their schools to feed and attract butterflies. These mini-habitats offer important food and refuge for insects and birds, especially during their migrations.

Many similar activities are under way all across the country. In the long run, the Neal Smith Refuge's main role may not be just to create a new prairie. It may be to encourage others to get involved in their own projects to help heal our earth. Already, about 150,000 people visit the refuge each year, including 20,000 schoolchildren. Many of them go home to look for their own prairie remnants or plant their own prairie gardens.

Like the Regal Fritillary, the Neal Smith Refuge serves as a flagship or beacon. It warns us to stop destroying ecosystems and species. More important, it invites everyone to join in restoring the natural wealth and beauty of our precious planet.

Butterfly gardens allow students to help nature and view wildlife up-close.

# Butterflies Go to School!

Schools around the country find that butterfly gardens are an easy, fun way to provide food and shelter for many species of butterflies. Some schools, though, take the idea of habitat to a higher level. Willowbrook School near Chicago has planted its own prairie on property shared by the local school and park districts. Working with the Chicago Botanic Garden and Glenview Park District, schoolchildren planted dozens of species of native plants including beebalm, ironweed, blue vervain, and cardinal flower.

According to Willowbrook librarian Kay Weisman, the prairie has taught students about natural ecosystems and has even inspired kids to write poetry. The prairie has also been a big hit. Says student Brandon Stark, "I like the prairie garden because you can catch cool bugs there and it looks really nice in the spring." Fellow student Haley Mooney agrees. "It is a nice place to go after school in the fall. It is very colorful and peaceful."

Willowbrook's sister school Wescott has also planted its own prairie and has even conducted controlled burns to nourish the native plants to health. These prairie projects prove that native habitat can improve the lives of both wildlife and people.

TOP LEFT: Students Brandon Stark and Haley Mooney help keep Willowbrook's prairie weed-free.
LEFT: Students at Willowbrook School near Chicago have planted their own native prairie.

# *Prairie Readings and Sites*

BOOKS

Adelman, Charlotte, and Bernard Schwartz. *Prairie Directory of North America* (Lawndale, 2001).

Collard, Sneed B., III. *Butterfly Count* (Holiday House, 2002).

Patent, Dorothy Hinshaw. *Prairies* (Holiday House, 1996).

———. *Fire: Friend or Foe* (Clarion, 1998).

St. Antoin, Sara, ed. *Stories from Where We Live — The Great North American Prairie* (Milkweed Editions, 2001).

Wallace, Marianne D. *America's Prairies and Grasslands* (Fulcrum, 2001).


WEB SITES

Friends of the Prairie Learning Center, Neal Smith National Wildlife Refuge: www.tallgrass.org.

North American Butterfly Association: www.naba.org.

42eXplore: www.42explore.com/prairie.htm (great links to many prairie topics).

The Tallgrass Prairie Preserve (The Nature Conservancy): http://nature.org/wherewework/northamerica/states/oklahoma/preserves/tallgrass.html.

A herd of bison

# Glossary

biodiversity: the total number and variety of living species and ecosystems that live on earth; also refers to the genetic diversity of living things.

biologist: someone who studies living organisms.

biomass: the total amount of tissue a living plant or animal contains.

botanist: a person who studies plants.

coevolve: to change with something else over extremely long periods of time; for instance, as a prairie community changes, different animals coevolve, or change, with it.

conservation biology: the field of science dedicated to learning about and protecting earth's species and ecosystems.

ecosystem: a community of plants, animals, and other organisms that depend on each other for survival.

evolution (to evolve): the very slow process by which species change over time and through which new species arise.

exotic species (plants, animals): species that are not native to a place or habitat; often these invaders displace or destroy native species.

forbs: flowering plants.

gene: the basic "instructions" of living things; they consist of pieces of DNA that define how cells and organisms grow and develop.

gravid: pregnant.

host plant: a plant that is crucial to the survival of an animal; for example, prairie violets are the host plants for the caterpillars of Regal Fritillary butterflies.

life cycle: the process from birth to death that an organism goes through during its lifetime.

parasites: organisms that live in or on another organism, or "host," extracting nutrition or other resources from the host, usually causing the host harm.

Ph.D.: a doctorate degree.

prairie: a grasslands ecosystem.

prairie remnant: a small piece of prairie, usually too small to support all of its original species.

reconstruction: the process of rebuilding from scratch an ecosystem that has been completely destroyed, as opposed to restoration.

restoration: the healing of an ecosystem that has been damaged but not completely destroyed.

savanna: an ecosystem that consists of mixed grasslands and open woodlands that allow a lot of light to reach the ground.

seedling: a newly sprouted plant or tree.

species: a distinct kind of plant, animal, or other living organism, usually defined as able to reproduce only with a member of its own species.

understory: the layer of plants that live under the shade or canopy of other plants, such as the trees of a savanna.

# Index

Monarch butterfly feeding on native prairie blazing star.